PORCUPINES

WILD ANIMALS OF THE WOODS

Lynn M. Stone

The Rourke Press, Inc.
Vero Beach, Florida 32964

PHOTO CREDITS
All photos © Lynn M. Stone except page 17 © Tom and Pat
Leeson

Library of Congress Cataloging-in-Publication Data

Stone, Lynn M.
　　Porcupines / Lynn Stone.
　　　　p. cm. — (Wild Animals of the woods)
　　Includes index.
　　ISBN 1-57103-092-1
　　1. North American porcupine—Juvenile literature.
[1. North American porcupine 2. Porcupines.] I. Title II. Series:
Stone, Lynn M. Wild Animals of the woods.
QL737.R652S748 1995
599.32' 34—dc20
　　　　　　　　　　　　　　　　　94–47386
　　　　　　　　　　　　　　　　　　CIP
　　　　　　　　　　　　　　　　　　AC

Printed in the USA

TABLE OF CONTENTS

PORCUPINES

The porcupine looks like a large, slow-moving pincushion. A porcupine isn't really armed with pins, but it does wear a coat of sharp quills on its tail and rump.

One porcupine may have as many as 30,000 quills. Each quill is actually a type of hollow hair.

Quills are not darts. A porcupine cannot throw them. To hurt an enemy, the porcupine has to slap it with its tail. Then the quills easily pull away from the porcupine and stick in the enemy.

A porcupine wears a coat of hair and quills

HOW THEY LOOK

A porcupine is more than a walking pincushion. Most of its upper body is covered by long, stiff hairs, not quills. The porcupine's belly is covered by woolly hair.

Porcupines have been known to weigh 35 pounds. They usually weigh from 10 to 12 pounds.

Like its cousin the beaver, a porcupine has a small head, small ears, short legs and a stocky body. Its feet have strong, sharply curved claws for climbing.

A porcupine reveals a tail and lower back full of quills

WHERE THEY LIVE

North American porcupines live throughout Alaska, Canada and the western United States. They also live in the Northeast.

Porcupines prefer a forest **habitat** (HAB uh tat), or home. But they are also found on Arctic **tundra** (TUN druh), desert, pastureland and along some grassy shores.

Porcupines spend much of their time on the ground, although they are fine climbers. They sometimes climb into a tree to take a nap.

Porcupines climb trees for naps and for some of their food

HOW THEY ACT

Porcupines may be active at day or night and in all seasons. Porcupines retreat to a hollow log or burrow only in the worst weather.

A porcupine doesn't walk far or fast, and it climbs trees slowly. But it sometimes climbs to heights of 55 feet.

Porcupines don't have keen eyes. They depend upon sharp hearing and a good sense of smell.

Porcupines make several noises, including grunts, coughs and tooth chattering.

A porcupine gnaws an antler for the minerals in it

Long hairs, rather than quills, cover most of a "porky," including its face and ears

PREDATOR AND PREY

Porcupines live almost totally upon plant matter. Depending upon the time of year, porcupines eat roots, leaves, bark, evergreen tree needles, berries and nuts.

Porcupines gnaw bones and antlers for the minerals in them. They also chow oar and tool handles because of the salty taste from human sweat.

Porcupines are **prey** (PRAY) for mountain lions, bobcats, wolverines, coyotes and fishers. These large **predators** (PRED uh tors), or hunters, flip porcupines onto their backs to avoid quills.

Porcupines eat tasty wild rose berries each autumn

PORCUPINE BABIES

A porcupine mother usually has just one baby, which she bears in the spring.

A newborn porcupine's quills are soft, but they harden within an hour of birth.

A baby porcupine can walk almost immediately. Within several days it can follow its mother up a tree.

Porcupines have lived to be 18 years old. They are more likely to reach seven or eight.

Porcupine babies soon have hard, sharp quills like their parents

THE PORCUPINE'S COUSINS

Porcupines are **rodents** (RO dents). The best known rodents are rats and mice. But mammals, such as squirrels, marmots and beavers, are also rodents.

Rodents have special front teeth—an upper and lower pair—that are ideal for gnawing. Since these teeth keep growing, rodents have to gnaw to keep the teeth worn down.

The smallest rodents weigh less than one ounce. The largest North American rodent, the beaver, can top 100 pounds!

The porcupine's cousin, the marmot, looks much like a porcupine without quills

PORCUPINES AND PEOPLE

People have had an ongoing interest in porcupines. Native Americans used porcupine quills in jewelry. They also ate porcupines, as did many pioneers.

Some people still eat porcupines. For someone lost in the woods, a slow-moving porcupine can be a lifesaving meal.

Porcupines are killed in certain areas because they gnaw tools, oars, saddles and even outdoor furniture.

Porcupine quills stick in a glove, wisely worn by someone who picked up a porcupine

THE PORCUPINE'S FUTURE

The porcupine's taste for tree bark sometimes kills the tree. That habit has caused the porcupine to be hunted and wiped out in some places. Loss of habitat has also reduced porcupine numbers, especially in the Northeast and upper Midwest.

In most areas, though, the porcupine continues to waddle along, its future quite safe.

Glossary

habitat (HAB uh tat) — the kind of place in which an animal lives, such as desert

predator (PRED uh tor) — an animal that kills another for food

prey (PRAY) — an animal that is hunted by another for food

rodent (RO dent) — any one of a large group of gnawing mammals, such as rats, mice and ground squirrels

tundra (TUN druh) — the low-lying, treeless plant cover of huge areas of the Far North

INDEX